WATSON, Sheila Elizab... HUMBE[R]

20. OCT 1995	18 DEC 2	
18. DEC. 1995	2 4 FEB 20[01]	1 9 OCT 2009
15. APR 1996	2 5 MAY 2001	
-4. OCT. 1996	3 0 AUG 2001	6 MAR 2010
26. OCT. 1996		
18. NOV 1996	2 0 APR 2002	
14. DEC. 1996		
14. DEC. 1998		
12. JUN 1999		
23. OCT. 1999		
14 OCT 2000		

WITHDRAWN

ALS No. B28838123 8

This item should be returned on or before the last date stamped above. If not in demand it may be renewed for a further period by personal application, by telephone, or in writing. The author, title, above number and date due back should be quoted. LS/3

9420055092.

KINGS ✤ AND ✤ QUEENS

Elizabeth I

Sheila Watson

Wayland

Titles in the series

Elizabeth I
Henry VIII
James VI/I
Mary Queen of Scots
Queen Victoria
William I

Series editor: Sarah Doughty
Book editor: Katie Orchard
Consultant: Mark Dartford
Designer: Jean Wheeler
Picture researcher: Liz Moore
Production controller: Carol Stevens

First published in 1995 by Wayland (Publishers) Ltd
61 Western Road, Hove, East Sussex BN3 1JD, England

© Copyright 1995 Wayland (Publishers) Ltd

British Library Cataloguing in Publication Data
Watson, Sheila
Elizabeth I – (Kings & Queens series)
I. Title II. Series
942.055092

ISBN 0 7502 1449 X

Typeset by Jean Wheeler
Printed and bound in Milan, Italy, by Rotolito Lombarda S.p.A.

Cover: A portrait of Elizabeth I in all her splendour.

Picture acknowledgements:
Ancient Art & Architecture Collection 11; Bodleian Library 16; British Library 14, 21 (top); Bridgeman Art Library *title page* (Trustees of Berkeley Castle), 4 (Museum of London), 7 (top) Fitzwilliam Museum, Cambridge, 18 (Private Collection), 19 (photograph by John Bethell), 25 (top) Philip Mould, (bottom) St Faith's Church, King's Lynn, 28 (Burghley House, Lincolnshire); B T Batsford 27 (right); Mary Evans 13 (top); E T Archive 5 (bottom), 20 (right), 27 (left); Robert Harding 7 (bottom); Andrew Hayden *back cover*; Hulton Deutsch 5 (top), 6, 8, 9 (top), 29 (top); Mansell 15 (bottom); Marquess of Salisbury 23 (right); National Maritime Museum 24; National Trust 10, 17; Plymouth City Museum and Art Gallery Collection 20 (left); Victoria and Albert Museum 9 (bottom). Commissioned photography on page 13 (bottom) is by Niall McLeod. All remaining pictures are from the Wayland Picture Library.

Contents

✤ The Early Years 4 ✤

✤ Elizabeth in Danger 10 ✤

✤ Queen at Last 14 ✤

✤ Triumphs and Troubles 20 ✤

✤ Decline 26 ✤

Glossary 30

Further Information 31

Index 32

The Early Years

IMPORTANT DATES

1509 *Henry VIII becomes King of England.*

Henry VIII marries Catherine of Aragon.

1516 *Mary Tudor is born.*

1533 *Henry marries Anne Boleyn.*

Henry and Catherine's marriage is declared non-existent.

Elizabeth is born.

1534 *Act of Parliament agrees that Henry is Supreme Head of the Church of England.*

Crowds cheered as Elizabeth I went in procession through the city of London on the day before her **coronation** in January 1559. Seated on a **litter**, wearing a long cloak of gold tissue, the young Queen was showered with **nosegays** and bunches of herbs. After her coronation, a great banquet was held in Westminster Hall.

Elizabeth I wearing her crown.

The Early Years

Elizabeth appearing in front of her people before her coronation.

The Queen's champion, Sir Edward Dymoke, offered to fight anyone who challenged Elizabeth's right to the throne. No one did, but many people there must have wondered at the fact that the second daughter of Henry VIII had lived to become Queen at twenty-five years of age. Few people could have realized that they were witnessing the beginning of one of the greatest reigns in history.

Elizabeth I was to face and overcome many threats and dangers and, finally, to die in 1603 a much-loved and respected monarch. However, when she became Queen in 1558, she had great problems to deal with – little money, religious disagreements, her rival Mary Queen of Scots, the threat of foreign attacks and her need to prove that she could rule England at a time when men gave the orders and women were expected to obey them. Elizabeth was fortunate. She was intelligent and learnt quickly. Above all, her early life had been hard and had taught her how to survive.

Elizabeth's champion, Sir Edward Dymoke, who was prepared to fight anyone who refused to accept her as Queen.

Elizabeth I

Anne Boleyn, Elizabeth's mother. This picture is from a drawing by Holbein, a German artist who was court painter to Henry VIII.

Anna Bollein Queen.

IMPORTANT DATES

1536 Anne Boleyn is executed.

Henry marries Jane Seymour.

1537 Edward is born.

1540 Henry marries Anne of Cleves and, later that year, has the marriage **annulled**.

Henry marries Catherine Howard.

1542 Catherine Howard is executed.

1543 Henry marries Catherine Parr.

1547 Henry VIII dies and Edward VI becomes King.

Everyone hoped that Elizabeth would be born a boy. **Astrologers** told her parents, Henry VIII and Anne Boleyn, to expect a prince. Elizabeth's birth on 7 September 1533 was a great disappointment. Henry already had a daughter, Mary, by his first wife Catherine of Aragon. Catherine was unable to have more children. Henry needed a son, for he was afraid that if a woman ruled after him, a male rival might try to take the throne from her. Against the Pope's wishes, Henry married Anne Boleyn and then had his marriage to Catherine declared non-existent. Although Henry kept Catholic worship, he became Supreme Head of the Church in England instead of the Pope.

Henry treated his new daughter well at first, hoping that Anne's next child would be a boy. Although

The Early Years

Henry VIII, Elizabeth's father, painted at about the time when he fell in love with Anne Boleyn, in around 1526.

The Old Palace, Hatfield House, where Elizabeth stayed as a child.

Elizabeth was brought up away from court, she was given much care and attention. Her mother made sure that she was dressed in fashionable clothes made of richly embroidered materials. Unfortunately, Anne **miscarried** the male child Henry wanted so much. She was not given another chance. Accused of having affairs with other men, she was **executed** on 19 May 1536, when Elizabeth was only two and a half years old. Elizabeth was declared **illegitimate** by an Act of Parliament. Her future was not at all certain.

Henry VIII married Jane Seymour only days after Anne's death. Elizabeth had little time to get used to her new stepmother, for Jane died soon after giving birth to Elizabeth's half-brother Edward, in 1537. She had three more stepmothers in a short space of time – Anne of Cleves, whose marriage to Henry VIII was

Elizabeth when she was about thirteen years old. Notice the books which show how much she loved studying.

The Early Years

annulled, Catherine Howard, who was executed, and Catherine Parr, who outlived the King. Although she rarely saw her father, she admired him and was always careful to try and please him. He was a powerful and magnificent man. Elizabeth learnt not to speak about her mother.

For the next few years, Elizabeth was brought up away from court, sometimes meeting her sister Mary and her brother Edward. She grew very fond of Edward, and she sometimes shared his lessons. As a child of the **Renaissance**, she was taught Latin and Greek, and she learnt to speak French and Italian very well. She was musical and learnt to play the **lute** and the **virginals**. Her tutors preferred **Protestant** ideas, and Elizabeth was not taught Catholic beliefs. However, she received no training in government, because Edward was to be King and her own future was not clear.

Roger Ascham, who taught Elizabeth ancient Greek and Latin.

Elizabeth was with her brother when he heard that Henry VIII had died. They wept together at the loss of their father. Edward became King Edward VI of England at only nine years old.

Elizabeth was musical and once owned these virginals.

Elizabeth in Danger

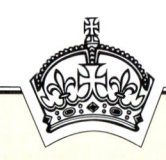

IMPORTANT DATES

1549 Thomas Seymour is sent to the Tower of London.

Seymour is executed.

1553 Edward VI dies.

Lady Jane Grey is proclaimed Queen.

Mary Tudor becomes Queen Mary I.

1554 Lady Jane Grey is executed.

(Right) The family tree of the kings and queens of England and Scotland. It shows the dates of their reigns and how Lady Jane Grey was linked to the royal family.

Edward VI, who reigned from 1547–53.

At first, the young King was controlled by his uncle, Edward Seymour. Seymour's brother Thomas was jealous, and he planned to marry Elizabeth to gain power for himself. Thomas was arrested, and Elizabeth was also in great danger if the Council could prove that she had agreed to his plans. She convinced her questioners that she had never intended to marry him. Thomas was executed, but Elizabeth was allowed to live.

After Henry VIII's **Reformation**, English rulers could establish whatever religion they chose, and English people had to accept that faith. King Edward VI set up a Protestant Church in England.

Elizabeth in Danger

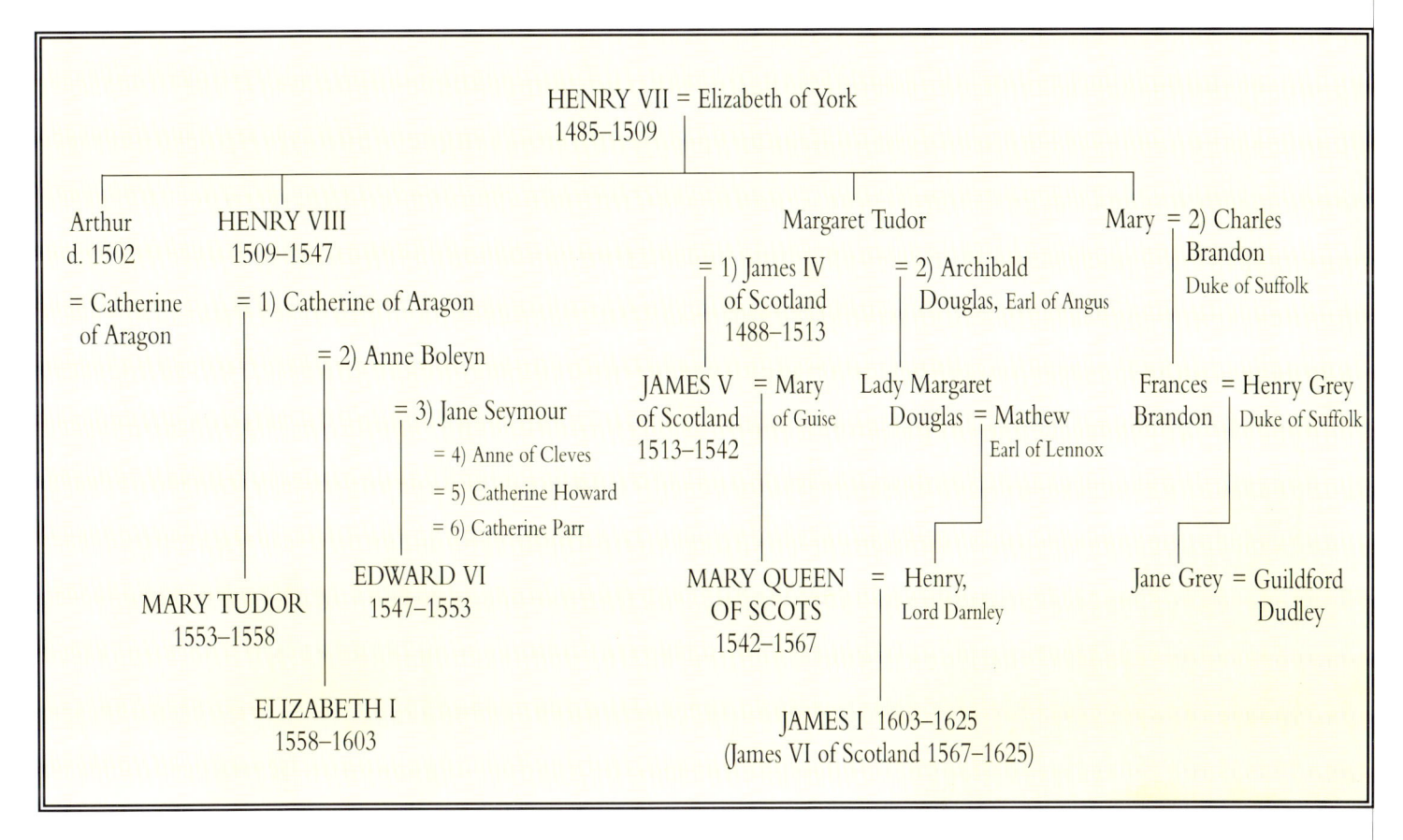

```
                        HENRY VII = Elizabeth of York
                              1485–1509
    ┌──────────┬──────────────┬─────────────────────────┬──────────────┐
 Arthur    HENRY VIII                      Margaret Tudor          Mary = 2) Charles
 d. 1502   1509–1547                                                     Brandon
                                 = 1) James IV    = 2) Archibald         Duke of Suffolk
 = Catherine  = 1) Catherine of Aragon  of Scotland    Douglas, Earl of Angus
   of Aragon                      1488–1513
              = 2) Anne Boleyn
                                JAMES V   = Mary     Lady Margaret      Frances = Henry Grey
                                of Scotland  of Guise  Douglas = Mathew   Brandon  Duke of Suffolk
              = 3) Jane Seymour 1513–1542                      Earl of Lennox
                  = 4) Anne of Cleves
                  = 5) Catherine Howard
                  = 6) Catherine Parr
                                   MARY QUEEN   = Henry,           Jane Grey = Guildford
  MARY TUDOR     EDWARD VI         OF SCOTS       Lord Darnley                  Dudley
  1553–1558      1547–1553         1542–1567

              ELIZABETH I               JAMES I  1603–1625
              1558–1603              (James VI of Scotland 1567–1625)
```

Mary Tudor would be Queen next if Edward died childless, and Mary was determined to restore the **Roman Catholic** religion in England. When Edward died young, his chief adviser, the Duke of Northumberland, tried to prevent this and to keep power for himself. He made his Protestant daughter-in-law, Lady Jane Grey, Queen. Elizabeth remained out of the way until she heard that her sister Mary was advancing on London. Jane, Queen for only nine days, was imprisoned and later executed. Elizabeth went to welcome Mary as Queen.

Elizabeth was next in line to the throne, and she knew that if she became in any way involved in similar plots against Mary, her life would also be in danger.

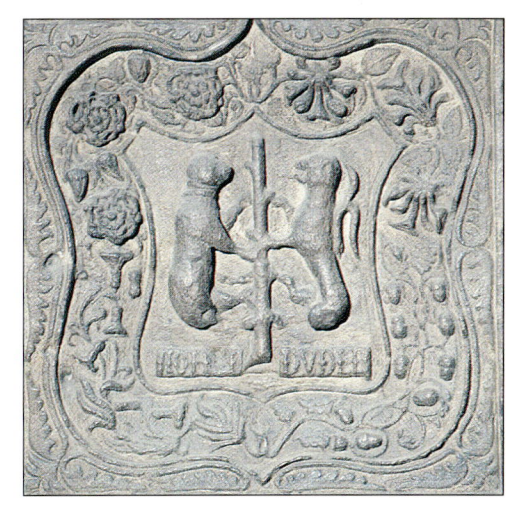

A carving in the Tower of London made by John Dudley. He and his four brothers were imprisoned there after his father, the Duke of Northumberland, tried to put Lady Jane Grey on the throne.

Elizabeth I

Mary Tudor aged twenty-eight, before she became Queen.

IMPORTANT DATES

1554 *Wyatt's rebellion.*

Elizabeth is imprisoned briefly in the Tower of London.

Sir Thomas Wyatt is executed.

Mary marries King Philip II of Spain.

1555 *Beginning of the burning of Protestants.*

Mary was determined to make England a Roman Catholic country again. She forced Elizabeth to attend Roman Catholic services, but suspected that Elizabeth remained a Protestant at heart. This angered Mary, for Elizabeth would undo all Mary's religious changes if she became Queen.

When Mary decided to marry King Philip II of Spain, many people were horrified. They hated the idea of England being part of Spain's empire. In desperation, Sir Thomas Wyatt and others tried to overthrow Mary and put Elizabeth on the throne.

Elizabeth in Danger

The rebellion failed, and Elizabeth was sent to the Tower of London. She went protesting her innocence to her escort. Over the next few weeks she waited for the order for her execution, but it never came. Wyatt was executed, but there was no proof that Elizabeth had become involved. Finally, Elizabeth was released.

Mary never had a child, although at least twice she thought she was pregnant. She burnt almost 300 Protestants trying to persuade people to accept the Roman Catholic faith but, as she lay dying, she knew that she had failed. Her Protestant sister had succeeded her.

Wyatt was beheaded after the failure of his rebellion against Mary.

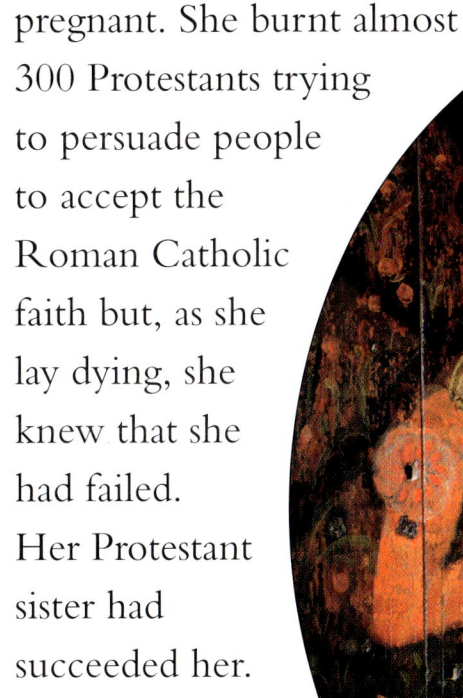

Queen Elizabeth's arrest. This is a painting on a wooden door from the Manor House at Little Gaddesden, Hertfordshire.

Queen at Last

Elizabeth was at Hatfield when she heard that Mary had died. She was twenty-five years old and was convinced that God had chosen her to be Queen. She said, 'This is the doing of the Lord; and it is marvellous in our eyes'. Although women were expected to take second place to men, Elizabeth always made it clear that she was the ruler of England. She listened to advice, but she alone took the decisions. She loved power. Years of living with an uncertain future had made her careful and wise.

Important Dates

1558 Elizabeth becomes Queen Elizabeth I of England.

1559 Elizabeth I is crowned Queen of England.

Elizabeth sets up a Protestant Church in England, with herself as Supreme Governor.

1560 Amy Robsart, Robert Dudley's wife, is found dead.

1579 Francis, Duke of Alençon, secretly comes to England for the first time, to try and marry Elizabeth.

1581–82 The Duke of Alençon returns to England.

Elizabeth sits alone while her counsellors stand respectfully to one side.

Queen at Last

Elizabeth recognized that she had a great responsibility to her people and she loved them. Most people adored and trusted her. Wherever she went, they cheered her and she would speak to even the humblest of her subjects.

Elizabeth had many problems to face. The country was divided over the question of religion. Mary's attempts to restore England to the Roman Catholic faith had left much bitterness. Protestants quarrelled over what sort of church they wanted Elizabeth to set up. England was a small, weak country compared to the powers of Spain and France. There was always the danger of foreign attacks. There was also the threat of Mary Queen of Scots, who might try to take the English throne. Finally, there was the question of Elizabeth's marriage. Who was she to marry, and when?

Elizabeth's signature. 'R' stands for regina, which is Latin for 'queen'.

Nonsuch Palace, one of Elizabeth's houses. This is the house she is supposed to have liked best.

Elizabeth I

William Cecil, Lord Burghley.

Parliament had little of the power it has today, but although Elizabeth took all the important decisions herself, she relied on the **Privy Council** and her **ministers** to advise her. The council looked after the routine government and administration of the country on Elizabeth's behalf. The most important person was her **Secretary of State**, William Cecil, later given the title Lord Burghley. He knew almost everything that was going on and helped her with her meetings, **correspondence** and foreign and financial affairs. Elizabeth trusted him more than any other person. They worked together for forty years.

Elizabeth set up a Protestant Church in England, and she hoped that everyone would belong to it. This was important because people were supposed to have the same religion as their monarch. If they had different beliefs, there was a danger that they might plot to overthrow and replace the ruler with someone of their own faith. Elizabeth's Church was very **moderate**, and most people attended services on Sundays. Anyone who refused to attend Church on Sundays and holy days could be fined. A few **Puritans** tried unsuccessfully to make the Church more to their liking. Some Roman Catholic priests who came to England to spread their faith were hunted down. If caught, they were sometimes **tortured** and executed.

A priest's hole in Oxburgh Hall. Roman Catholic priests would use special hiding places like this one to hide from government officials if they came searching for them.

Elizabeth I

Elizabeth dancing with Robert Dudley.

No one believed Elizabeth when she said that she was **reluctant** to get married. She was expected to find a husband who would help her with the cares and responsibilities of government. She also needed a **legitimate** child, because she was the last of the children of Henry VIII. However, Elizabeth was unwilling to share her power with anyone.

She had many proposals of marriage, including one from her brother-in-law, King Philip II, who wanted to keep England under Spanish influence. She refused him, but several times her courtiers thought she might marry. Robert Dudley, Earl of Leicester, made her laugh and went hunting with her, and for a time she seemed to love him.

Unfortunately, he was married. When his wife Amy died from a fall down some stairs, he was suspected of her murder. Elizabeth could never marry him after that.

Several times, Elizabeth talked of marrying a Catholic French prince, Francis, Duke of Alençon who was much younger than she was. She needed the friendship of France and she liked her 'frog', as she called him. He came to England twice to win her hand, secretly at first in 1579, and then again, in 1581–82. However, her advisers and the public were afraid of possible French and Catholic influence in England. Elizabeth died unmarried, and without a child of her own to succeed her.

Kenilworth Castle, Warwickshire, as it is today. Originally, it was the home of Robert Dudley, Earl of Leicester. Elizabeth stayed here for eighteen days in 1575.

Triumphs and Troubles

Elizabeth I admired and rewarded people who had the courage to risk their lives and fortunes in exploring the world. She sometimes **invested** in their **expeditions**, because she liked the idea that such adventures weakened the power of the Spanish King, Philip II, who had a great empire. She also expected a share in their profits. Francis Drake, an explorer, made a great voyage round the world in his ship *The Golden Hind* in 1577–80. He brought back treasure and jewels taken from Spanish ships. Elizabeth was given a large amount of the wealth, and she had him knighted.

At home, Elizabeth enjoyed going on **progress** in the summer when she would travel round the country

(Above) Drake's cup which celebrates Drake's round-the-world voyage. The model of the world opens on a hinge.

(Right) Ceremonies and processions were an important part of court life.

Elizabeth I travelling round the country. The winged figure of Fame shows how well known she was. Notice how she travels in an open carriage so everyone can see her.

with her court, allowing herself to be seen by her people and being entertained. In London or on progress, she was always surrounded by her advisers and those who hoped for favour and promotion, and by her ladies-in-waiting who looked after her comfort. Elizabeth frequently watched plays, and William Shakespeare's *Twelfth Night* was performed at court in 1601. She loved dancing and music, and also liked hunting, **bear-baiting** and watching tournaments. Poets called her 'Gloriana' and she encouraged the idea that she was special. This set her apart and made her more powerful.

IMPORTANT DATES

1568 *Mary Queen of Scots flees to England.*

1570 *Pope excommunicates Elizabeth, releasing all English Roman Catholics from their loyalty to her.*

1577–80 *Francis Drake sails round the world in* The Golden Hind.

1587 *Mary Queen of Scots is executed at Fotheringhay Castle.*

1588 *Defeat of the Spanish Armada.*

Elizabeth I

A medal, made of lead, showing Mary Queen of Scots after she had become a prisoner of Elizabeth I.

Elizabeth I distrusted Mary Queen of Scots. Mary was a Roman Catholic. Some people believed that she had a better right to the English throne than Elizabeth, because Roman Catholics did not feel that Henry VIII's marriage to Elizabeth's mother, Anne Boleyn, was legal.

Mary was a big enough problem for Elizabeth in France (where she had, for a short time, been Queen) and in her own country, Scotland, but she was an even greater threat to her when she arrived in England asking for help against her rebellious subjects.

Some Roman Catholics, encouraged by the Pope, plotted to put Mary on the throne of England. Elizabeth's advisers often urged her to execute Mary, but she did not want to kill a fellow Queen who had sought her help. She refused to allow Mary to go abroad, and instead kept her under guard in various castles and houses for almost nineteen years. During that time, several of Mary's supporters were caught and executed for plotting to place her on the English throne. However, most Catholics remained loyal to Elizabeth.

Triumphs and Troubles

Elizabeth always tried to appear richly dressed like this in public. Her clothes are decorated with fine needlwork and jewels.

(Below) The order for the execution of Mary Queen of Scots.

Finally, it was proved that Mary had agreed to a plan to kill Elizabeth. Reluctantly, Elizabeth agreed to Mary's execution at Fotheringhay Castle in February 1587, although she was angry that Mary should have such a public execution. King Philip had already decided to attack England, and the news only made him more determined to destroy Elizabeth.

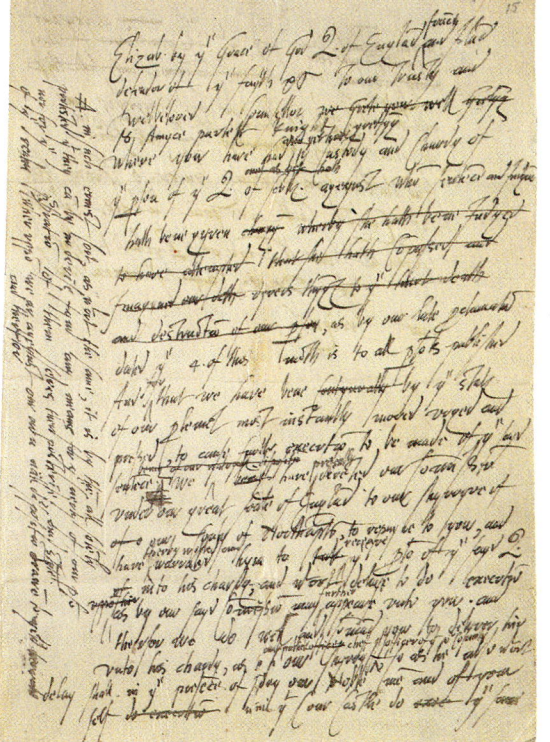

English ships fighting the Spanish Armada.

Elizabeth disliked war. She was afraid that more powerful countries might attack her, so she tried to weaken them. She helped Protestants in France against their Catholic King and sent troops to help the Dutch when they rebelled against their Spanish masters. She also allowed English sailors to attack Spanish ships for gold and silver. Philip II of Spain had once offered to marry Elizabeth, but her actions made him determined to remove her from her throne.

In 1588, Philip sent a great fleet of 130 ships, the Armada, full of soldiers, to escort more soldiers from the Netherlands and invade England. Leicester

Triumphs and Troubles

gathered together an army and Elizabeth sent her fleet to attack the approaching ships. Her country was united behind her and she went down to Tilbury in person, to address her troops. She inspired them all by her words, 'I am come amongst you...being resolved...to live or die amongst you all, to lay down for my God and for my kingdom and for my people, my honour and my blood, even in the dust...' At sea, the English fleet attacked the enemy ships until the great Armada was driven northwards by the wind. The danger passed and Elizabeth returned to London to be greeted by adoring crowds. It was her moment of triumph. She was never to be so popular again.

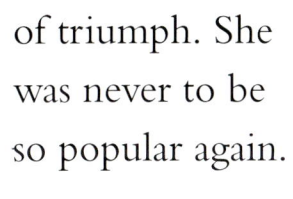

Philip II of Spain, Elizabeth's brother-in-law. He was determined to have Elizabeth removed from the throne.

Elizabeth riding to Tilbury to speak to her troops. In the top part of the picture, she gives thanks for her victory.

Decline

The years after the Armada were difficult for Elizabeth. Many of her friends and advisers died: Leicester in 1588, Walsingham (a minister), in 1590, and Burghley in 1598. Elizabeth went to Burghley's house to feed him herself with a spoon, in an attempt to make him strong, but she could not keep him alive. Younger, less experienced men replaced her old advisers at court.

One of these, the Earl of Essex, had charmed her with his good looks and his flattery. He was young and bold, and she sent him to control a rebellion in Ireland. He failed and, in disgrace, he lost his power and wealth. Fearing he had lost her favour for good, deep in debt and desperate, he tried to raise the citizens of London in an uprising against her. She was too popular, and he failed to win support. He paid the price for **treason** with his life. Elizabeth was greatly distressed at having to order his execution, but she could not let a **traitor** live.

The Earl of Essex, Elizabeth's last favourite, who was later executed for treason.

Decline

(Above) Poor people were often treated harshly in Elizabeth's time. Beggars were whipped through the streets.

(Left) Elizabeth I and Parliament.

Important Dates

1588 Robert Dudley, Earl of Leicester, Elizabeth's favourite dies.

1590 Sir Francis Walsingham dies.

1598 William Cecil, Lord Burghley dies.

1599 Earl of Essex leads an expedition to Ireland.

1601 Essex rebellion. Essex is executed for treason.

1603 Elizabeth I dies. James VI of Scotland becomes James I of England.

War with Spain dragged on and taxes were high, in order to pay for troops. Meanwhile, the harvests of 1594–98 were poor, and some people went hungry in parts of England. Elizabeth needed Parliament to vote for taxes and pass certain laws, but Parliament became more critical of some of the Queen's policies.

Elizabeth I in old age, dressed as magnificently as ever.

Even when Elizabeth was old and ill, she took great care to look impressive, because it was important for her to appear strong and powerful. She wore beautiful dresses and a red wig. She could not, however, hide her yellow teeth, sunken eyes and wrinkled neck. She became increasingly depressed and tired of life.

In March 1603, she became so ill that she ate and slept very little, sitting up all night on cushions on the floor. Finally, she was persuaded to go to bed. In the

Decline

early hours of the morning of 24 March, a messenger rode north to tell King James VI of Scotland, the only son of Mary Queen of Scots, that he was now King of England as well.

After Elizabeth's death, she regained much of her lost popularity. People forgot her bad tempers and her reluctance to make up her mind. They remembered her as the wise, powerful monarch who had courageously organized the defence of her kingdom, and who had, above all, cared for the people she ruled. As Elizabeth once said, when speaking to Members of Parliament at Whitehall Palace, 'And though you have had, and may have, many Princes, more mighty and wise sitting in this state, yet you never had or shall have any that will be more careful and loving.'

James VI of Scotland, who became James I of England on the death of Elizabeth.

Elizabeth's funeral procession.

Glossary

Act of Parliament A law which is passed in Parliament.

annulled Cancelled, or made invalid.

astrologers People who claim to be able to tell the future by studying the stars.

bear-baiting Bears fighting dogs for sport.

coronation The church service when someone is crowned king or queen.

correspondence Written communications.

executed When someone has been killed as a punishment.

expeditions Long journeys.

illegitimate Someone whose parents were not married when he or she was born.

invest To support a scheme in the hope of gaining something in return. Queen Elizabeth I sometimes invested ships in overseas expeditions.

legitimate Someone whose parents were married when he or she was born.

litter A couch on which a person was carried.

lute A musical instrument like a guitar.

minister The name given to an adviser to the Queen, who had a special government job to do.

miscarried Gave birth to a child too early so it was born dead.

moderate Not extreme.

nosegays Small bunches of flowers which could be held in the hand and smelt.

Privy Council A group of important men who advised the Queen.

progress The official name of Elizabeth's summer tours.

Protestant A Christian person who does not accept the Pope as the Head of the Christian Church.

Puritans Members of the Church of England who wanted to make it less like the Roman Catholic Church.

Reformation A move to change the Catholic Church which reduced the Pope's power.

reluctant Not willing to do something.

Renaissance A time of new ideas in art and learning which had their origins in the study of classical learning.

Roman Catholic Someone who believes the Pope is the Head of the Christian Church, and who obeys the Pope's religious laws.

Secretary of State The King or Queen's most important adviser and minister.

torture To make someone feel great pain.

traitor A person who betrays his or her country to an enemy.

treason Plotting against the King or Queen.

virginals A musical instrument with a keyboard – a little like a small piano.

Further Information

Books to Read

A World of Change by R. Kelly (Stanley Thornes Ltd, 1987)

Mary Queen of Scots by D. Turner (Wayland, 1988. Reprinted in 1994)

Queen Elizabeth I by D. Turner (Wayland, 1987. Reprinted in 1994)

Queen of Scots by F. Macdonald (Piccolo, 1994)

Tudor and Stuart Chronicle by J. Mason (Longman, 1993)

Tudors by D. Bailey (Headway, 1993)

Tudors and Stuarts by D. Cooper and B. Cliftlands (BBC, 1993)

Places to Visit

Buckland Abbey, Yelverton, Devon.
The home of Sir Francis Drake from 1581.

Burghley House, Stamford, Lincolnshire.
The home of William Cecil, Lord Burghley.

Hardwick Hall, Near Chesterfield, Derbyshire.
Built by Bess of Hardwick in 1591–97.

Hatfield House, Hatfield, Hertfordshire.
Elizabeth spent much of her childhood in the old Royal Palace of Hatfield, part of which survives in the grounds today.

Hever Castle, near Edenbridge, Kent.
The childhood home of Elizabeth's mother, Anne Boleyn.

Palace of Holyroodhouse, Edinburgh.
One of Mary Queen of Scots' homes in Scotland.

Jedburgh, Borders.
Mary Queen of Scots' house. Contains her communion set and other items once belonging to her.

Kenilworth Castle, Kenilworth, Warwickshire.
Now a grand ruin, once the home of the Earl of Leicester where he entertained Elizabeth for eighteen days in 1575.

National Portrait Gallery, St Martin's Place, London.
Contains portraits of Elizabeth and some of her contemporaries.

Tower of London, Tower Hill, London.
Once both a prison and a royal palace.

Westminster Abbey, London.
Contains Elizabeth I's tomb, as well as that of Mary Queen of Scots.

Index

Figures in **bold** refer to illustrations. Glossary entries are shown by the letter g.

Alençon, Duke of 19, **19**
Anne of Cleves 8
Armada 24-25, **24**
Ascham, Roger **9**
astrologers 6, 30g

Boleyn, Anne 6, **6**, 7
Burghley, Lord (*see Cecil, William*)

Catherine of Aragon 6
Cecil, William 16, **16**, 26
champions 5, **5**
coronation 5, **5**

Drake, Sir Francis 20
Dudley, Robert 18-19, **18**, 26
Dymoke, Sir Edward 5, **5**

education 9
Edward VI 8, 9, 10
entertainment 21
Essex, Earl of 26, **26**
executions 7, 9, 10, 13, 17, 23, 26, 30g
expeditions 20, 30g

Golden Hind, The 20
Grey, Lady Jane 11

Hatfield House **7**, 14
Henry VIII 5, 6-7, **7**, 8, 22
Howard, Catherine 9

James VI/I 29, **29**

Kenilworth Castle **19**

Leicester, Earl of (*see Dudley, Robert*)

Mary Queen of Scots 5, 15, 22-3, **22**, 29

Mary Tudor 6, 9, 10-12, **12**
miscarriages 7, 30g

Nonsuch Palace **15**
Northumberland, Duke of 11

Parliament 16, 27, **27**, 29
Parr, Catherine 9
Philip II of Spain 12, 18, 20, 23, 24-5, **25**
Pope 6, 22
Protestants 9, 10, 12, 13, 15, 24, 30g

Roman Catholics 6, 12, 13, 15, 22, 24

Seymour, Edward 10
Seymour, Jane 8
Seymour, Thomas 10

Wyatt, Sir Thomas 12-13, **13**